Contents

Acknowledgements

The publishers wish to express their gratitude to the following for permission to include copyright material in this book:

The Catholic Institute for International Relations, Unit 3, Canonbury Yard, 190a New North Road, Islington, London, N1 7BJ, for the quotation by Oscar Romero.

Darton, Longman & Todd Ltd, 1 Spencer Court, 140-142 Wandsworth High Street, London, SW18 4JJ, for the extract from *Good Friday People* by Sheila Cassidy, published and copyright 1991 by Darton, Longman & Todd Ltd.

HarperCollins Publishers Ltd, 77-85 Fulham Palace Road, Hammersmith, London, W6 8JB, for the quotation from *A Bible Prayer Book for Today* by Peter De Rosa.

SCM-Canterbury Press Ltd, 9-17 St Albans Place, London, N1 0NX for the extract from the poem 'Morning Prayers' from *Letters and Papers from Prison,* the Enlarged Edition, by Dietrich Bonhoeffer, 1971.

Syndication International Ltd, 4-12 Dorrington Street, London, EC1N 7TB, for the photograph 'Suddenly it's spring!'

All other photographs in the book are © Copyright UNWRA and used by permission.

Darton, Longman & Todd Ltd, and les Editions du Cerf for extracts from the New Jerusalem Bible, © 1985.

The Bible Societies/HarperCollins Publishers Ltd, UK, for the extract on pages 56-57 taken from the Good News Bible, © American Bible Society, 1966, 1971, 1976 and 1992. (The passage on page 39, Psalm 103 (102), is a translation by H. J. Richards.)

Every effort has been made to trace the owners of copyright material and we hope that no copyright has been infringed. Pardon is sought and apology made if the contrary be the case and a correction will be made in any reprint of this book.

Introduction

Lent has always been a time for reflection. It is a time to take stock and to check out if we are really living as followers of Jesus. This Lent we are guided by Luke, the evangelist who built his Gospel around the theme of 'journeys'. We are on a journey that is heading for Jerusalem and the cross. This is not going to be a comfortable ride.

This is not to say that it is all gloom and misery. After all, in Old English 'lencten' means spring. Lent is a time of hope, of new life and the promise of resurrection. But flowers don't bloom in the spring sunshine unless the bulbs are first buried deep in the dark soil and drenched in rain.

There are five chapters in this book because it has become an established custom for Lenten discussion groups to meet during the five weeks of Lent, but not during Holy Week. We have written this book together hoping that it will provide helpful material for individuals, for groups in parishes or for teachers for school assemblies.

Each chapter follows the same outline:

- The Gospel text for the Sunday
- A brief commentary by Bert
- Further reflections by Clare
- A summary
- Questions for discussion
- Suggestions for action
- A prayer

Bert and Clare Richards

A time of testing

Reading for the first Sunday of Lent

Filled with the Holy Spirit, Jesus left the Jordan and was led by the Spirit into the desert, for forty days being put to the test by the devil. During that time he ate nothing and at the end he was hungry. Then the devil said to him, 'If you are Son of God, tell this stone to turn into a loaf.' But Jesus replied, 'Scripture says: **Human beings live not on bread alone.**'

Then leading him to a height, the devil showed him in a moment of time all the kingdoms of the world and said to him, 'I will give you all this power and their splendour, for it has been handed over to me, for me to give it to anyone I choose. Do homage, then, to me, and it shall be all yours.' But Jesus answered him, 'Scripture says: **You must do homage to the Lord your God, him alone you must serve.**'

Then he led him to Jerusalem and set him on the parapet of the Temple. 'If you are Son of God,' he said to him, 'throw yourself down from here, for scripture says: He has given his angels orders about you, to guard you; and again: They will carry you in their arms in case you trip over a stone.'

But Jesus answered him, 'Scripture says: **Do not put the Lord your God to the test.**'

Having exhausted every way of putting him to the test, the devil left him, until the opportune moment.

Luke 4:1-13

Today is the first of the six Sundays of Lent.
Are these going to be six weeks of misery, or six weeks of mercy?
Six weeks of gloom, or of gladness?

Well, let's start with the gloomy bit.
In the Gospel reading, Jesus is being put to the test
    (that's a better word than 'tempted').
We're trying to find out what Jesus is made of.
And the testing lasts forty days, while Jesus is alone in the desert,
    without company and without food.
Of course, that is why we read the story today as we set out
    on our forty-day Lent journey,
    and try to do our bit of silent reflection and fasting.
Because this Lent will be a testing time for us too,
    to find out what *we're* made of.

Tests are nasty things.
We've all had them at school, from infancy through to college:
    questionnaires, orals, written papers, essays and exams.
We've all had them at the doctor's too,
    and those visits go on long after college days:
    jabs, samples, smears, X-rays and operations.
And, in both cases, waiting to hear the results has often been
    more nerve-wracking than the tests themselves.
How did we do? What marks did we get?

The test question that is put to Jesus three times is:
Are you *really* the Son of God?
And behind that question lie the deeper ones:
What sort of person would a real son of God be?
What would he stand for? What would his priorities be?
What would he try to do, and what never do?
How would he show he really *was* a son of God,
    a really godly person?
How would he try to establish the kingdom of God,
    where God could be seen as really being in charge,

and not hiding behind a screen?
Tough questions. How would we answer them?

The options that the devil puts to Jesus are very attractive ones.
The devil's not daft; what's a spoonful of sugar for?
After all, why *not* use your God-given powers to provide food for
the starving, not least yourself?
Moses didn't hesitate to do it for his people when *he* was in the
desert.
Who could fail to follow a Messiah like that?
Or, why not play along with the powers that be?
They may not be very savoury characters, but you can't get into
power standing on the sidelines.
Who would follow a Messiah who had no political clout?

Or, why not push the boat out and *force* God to show
he's on your side?
After all, one of the psalms says that's exactly what he'll do
for his friends.
Is Jesus unsure whether God *is* his friend?
And Jesus' answer to these attractive suggestions?
One, there's more to life than food.
Two, there's no meeting God half-way.
Three, there's no forcing God's hand.
Jesus' three answers are all quotations from the book of Deuteronomy,
which tells of Israel's long journey through the desert.
To show what a true Jew he was, Jesus begins his ministry by
reliving for forty days his people's arduous forty-year journey
to the Promised Land, where 'back to the fleshpots of Egypt' was
an attractive option.

And we shouldn't imagine that this was the only time
that Jesus felt attracted to taking the easy way out.
Our reading stands on the first page of the story of his public life.
But it's only a summary of a theme that will crop up again and again.

9

Look out for Peter's suggestion that Jesus shouldn't stir up trouble in
 Jerusalem, and the sharp reply: 'Get behind me, Satan!'
Look out for Gethsemane, where keeping faith with God meant
 sweating blood.
Look out for Calvary, where people thought being a son of God
 would get you out of trouble. It does the opposite.
Look out for Paul's reassurance that, as a weak human being just
 like us, Jesus was tempted *in every way* that we are (Hebrews 4:15).
Living a godly life in a world where 'Evil Rules OK' is no bed of
 roses; more like a crown of thorns.
We must keep this in mind, over these forty days of Lent.

Well, that's the gloomy bit, the bad news.
The glad bit, the good news, is that this time of testing
 is also a time of grace.
Do you know the Chinese word for 'crisis'?
It's written with two symbols:
 one means 'risk' and the other means 'opportunity'.
In other words, a time of crisis is a time when you're at risk.
You *could* come a cropper.
But you could equally well go forward another step.
Lent is such a time of crisis: it can be a golden opportunity.
Our reading has outlined Jesus as another son of God, like Adam,
 seizing the opportunity where the first Adam failed.
Sons and daughters of God, we walk these forty desert days
 holding the hand of our brother Jesus.

Further reflections

Some years ago I took part in a local Lenten broadcast as part of the Inter-Church Lent courses. I am reminded of this as I reflect on this week's Gospel passage and Bert's comments. We can so easily become too familiar with Gospel texts and fail to appreciate the original impact they made on the reader. In our broadcasts we decided to avoid this by trying to read the Gospel through someone else's eyes. We read and discussed the texts bearing in mind the lives of people whose experience of the world is very different from our own.

Take the text in today's Gospel where Jesus replies to the devil: 'Scripture says: *Human beings live not on bread alone*', or 'There's more to life than food'. This is rather an obvious truth for those of us who are able to enjoy several meals a day, have a good job, enough money for an active social life and the certainty of a secure future. What if you live in a rain-starved African desert or on the edge of a rubbish dump in São Paulo? For hungry people in many parts of the world today there is very little in life except the endless search for food. What do these people make of Jesus' reply?

I find myself saying to Jesus, 'Hold on a moment, starving people will find your words meaningless.' I am sensitive on this point because our twins were suffering from severe malnutrition when we adopted them in Colombia. Pedro (who weighed 4lb at seven months old!) was desperate for food in the early months of his life. It was such a joy to see his little face light up at meal times that Bert wrote the following 'interview' in the children's diary:

> 'Can you tell me, Pedro, what your first thought is on waking up?'
>   'Food.'
> 'And what is the first word you spoke?'
>   'Food.'
> 'What do you like about going to the shops with Mum?'
>   'Food.'
> 'What would you like for Christmas?'
>   'Food.'

11

'What do you think about when sitting in your push-chair?'
   'Food.'
'What industry do you hope to enter when you grow up?'
   'Food.'
'What is your last thought before you sleep?'
   'Food.'
'What do you dream about?'
   'Food.'

We were very amused when we came across these early scribblings recently, especially as our son is now a chef. But the fact is that malnutrition and hunger dominate the lives of the poor. What was Jesus saying to them? In our radio broadcast one of the members told the story of the people of Mombin Crochu in Haiti. A four-month period of the year in that region is known as 'hungry time'. The people eat only mangoes to keep hunger pangs at bay as they wait for the main harvest. Last year's corn, beans and cassava have been eaten and the best land is used to grow rice for export only. The hungry people need cash and have to sell most of the mangoes too. They get 50p for a basket of 200 mangoes. Weeks later these are sold in England for at least at £1 each.

The priest in Mombin Crochu must find it quite difficult to preach to his community during 'hungry time', especially on the Sunday when the Gospel reading is the 'Feeding of the five thousand' which concludes with the words *everyone got enough to eat*. On one Feast day as the communion plate was passed around, with small pieces of consecrated bread, he saw that the people were watching each other carefully. They were so hungry that they needed to make sure no one took two pieces. The priest proclaimed the words of Jesus: *'I am the bread of life. Whoever eats of me will never hunger.'*

We have to ask ourselves how we would feel on hearing these words, if we lived in Mombin Crochu. The fact is that the Christian faith is probably more alive and well in Latin America than it is here in Britain. Many people who live in great poverty find inspiration and encouragement by simply reading the Bible together in groups known as Basic Christian Communities. They read and question the Gospel texts and then take action to help each other. Their resolutions are practical and improve the life of the whole community. They reflect on their actions and bring into their liturgy a great joy and determination to live with a sense of God's presence in their daily struggling lives. I have no doubt that the Mombin Crochu communities responded vigorously to the challenge that 'there is more to life than food'.

Of course, their response may have involved political action of some kind. They may, for example, have voted for action against unfair farming practices. And this brings us to the second test that Jesus faced in the desert. The devil offered Jesus political success and power, which he rejected saying: '*You must do homage to the Lord your God, him alone you must serve.*' Some Christians read this text as confirmation that Jesus preached only a spiritual message; that he prepared us for the kingdom of God which is not related to this world of politics and daily life. They believe that political action is always inappropriate for Christians.

People who live in countries governed by corrupt dictators will not interpret this text in that way. They will most likely see that Jesus was rejecting the power and authority of autocratic rulers and embracing the rule of love and service of others. This has to involve challenging leaders who abuse their power, or rules which enslave and harm our neighbours. We are not unaware of this in our own circumstances. How quickly Christian voices would be raised if the government proposed to make abortion easier or encouraged schools to make contraceptives available for pupils. Would those same Christian voices be willing to challenge politicians over world hunger and global injustices? This Lent may be a very good time for us to examine our position and check how consistent (or not) our commitment to the Gospel really is.

The third 'temptation' or 'testing' that Luke describes in our Gospel text will surely be read by the people in Mombin Crochu as 'Don't expect miracles to happen – find a way to feed one another'. When Jesus quoted Deuteronomy by saying '*Do not put the Lord your God to the test'*, he was saying that we must solve our own problems and not expect divine intervention. Have you ever had to write the bidding prayers for your church liturgy? Isn't it difficult to word the prayers in such a way that it doesn't imply that we are simply handing over the needs to God? 'Dear Lord, help the hungry people in Haiti . . .' How? How is God going to help them?

As we start these forty days of Lent with Jesus at a crisis point in his life, it is worth considering those Chinese symbols that Bert described: *risk* and *opportunity*. Jesus embraced the opportunity to preach to his contemporaries about the kingdom of God but by so doing he risked upsetting the authorities. And he paid the price. What price am I prepared to pay?

Photograph: UNWRA

Tested by poverty and injustice.

14

Summary

The readings this Lent are taken from Luke's Gospel. The first reading, Luke 4:1-13, is a detailed account of Jesus being put to the test as he thought about the new direction his life should take. He spent forty days in the desert where the devil put three attractive suggestions before him. They seem reasonable enough but he rejects the ideas and responds with thoughts inspired by the writer of Deuteronomy:

> There's more to life than food.
> There's no meeting God half-way.
> There's no forcing God's hand.

Jesus refuses to take the easy path, and at this crisis in his life he grasps the *opportunity* to go out and preach the kingdom of God. In doing so he *risks* the displeasure of authorities, and we know that he will pay the price with his life.

It is sometimes a good idea to read the Gospel text through the eyes of people who live lives very different from our own. It can give a freshness to well-known stories and can take us by surprise. People in the developing world who are 'tested' by poverty and injustice may be able to tell us something new about the challenge of the Gospel.

Discussion points

1. What do you suppose Jesus meant by saying, 'Human beings live not on bread alone?' What else do they live on?

2. Jesus quoted Deuteronomy when he said, 'Do not put the Lord your God to the test'. Later he was to tell his disciples that if they 'asked' in prayer, they would 'receive'. Isn't that really putting God to the test too? How do you explain the incompatibility of the texts?

3. Reflect on the Chinese symbols for the word 'crisis'. One means risk, the other means 'opportunity'. It is sometimes said that the Church is in crisis today. What risks and opportunities should it take?

4. It would seem to be a miracle for the people of Mombin Crochu if they had enough food to eat throughout a whole year. How could this 'miracle' come about?

5. How politically involved should Christians become in issues of human rights, justice and peace? Find some backing from the Gospels for your view.

Suggestions for action

As Lent is a time for reflection and action (prayer, fasting and alms-giving) here are a few suggestions.

- **Prayer**
  Plan a short service for your group or parish based on world hunger.

- **Fasting**
  Plan a hunger lunch for CAFOD. Give up some time to find out more about human rights.

- **Almsgiving**
  Make a charity collection box for your family, group or parish and target a chosen issue for this Lenten project.

Prayer

To keep a true Lent

Is this a Fast, to keep
the Larder leane
and cleane
from fat of Veales and Sheep?

Is it to quit the dish
of Flesh, yet still
to fill
the platter high with Fish?

Is it to faste an houre,
or ragg'd to go,
or show
a downcast look, and sowre?

No: 'tis a Fast, to dole
thy sheaf of wheat
and meat
unto the hungry Soule.

It is to fast from strife
from old debate
and hate;
to circumcise thy life.

To shew a heart grief-rent;
to starve thy sin,
not Bin;
and that's to keep thy Lent.
Robert Herrick (1591-1674)

Week Two

Easter is ahead

Reading for the second Sunday of Lent

Now about eight days after this had been said, he took with him Peter, John and James and went up the mountain to pray. And it happened that, as he was praying, the aspect of his face was changed and his clothing became sparkling white. And suddenly there were two men talking to him; they were Moses and Elijah appearing in glory, and they were speaking of his passing which he was to accomplish in Jerusalem. Peter and his companions were heavy with sleep, but they woke up and saw his glory and the two men standing with him. As these were leaving him, Peter said to Jesus, 'Master, it is wonderful for us to be here; so let us make three shelters, one for you, one for Moses and one for Elijah.' He did not know what he was saying. As he was saying this, a cloud came and covered them with shadow; and when they went into the cloud the disciples were afraid. And a voice came from the cloud saying, 'This is my Son, the Chosen One. Listen to him.' And after the voice had spoken, Jesus was found alone. The disciples kept silence and, at that time, told no one what they had seen.

Luke 9:28-36

What a surprise, so early in Lent, to have this preview of Easter.
Why are we being shown the glorious and triumphant Risen Christ
    so soon?
After all, there are still another four weeks of Lent to go!
'Yes, but the journey is worthwhile', today's reading is telling us.
'Keep at it. The ending will take your breath away!'

Most pilgrims who make their way to the Holy Land
    manage to fit in a visit to Mount Tabor in Galilee.
No one knows exactly where the Transfiguration experience
    is supposed to have taken place.
Does it matter?
The story needed a place to be rooted in,
and the 1800 feet of Tabor – 'a high mountain apart' –
    makes a brilliant setting.
It is here that the Byzantines and the Crusaders erected a church,
    and the modern basilica that today crowns the summit
    is a prayerful (and wonderfully resounding) successor.

What is it that pilgrims sing about on Mount Tabor?
What exactly is it that the Gospel story is saying?
Is it trying to describe some external and objective event
    which any passing fell-walker could have witnessed?
Or is the story about something much more internal?

The Gospels speak of it as a 'vision',
    and they even speak of the three disciples as 'sleeping'.
Could this have been a dream they had?
Or are we dealing with a mystical experience
    enjoyed by Jesus himself?
Certainly Luke talks in these terms.
Five times he omits the references to the disciples made by Mark
    and Matthew.
Jesus goes up to the mountain not to exhibit his glory,
    but quite simply 'to pray'.
He repeats this twice.

The extraordinary transformation of Jesus –
    face shining like the sun,
    clothes whiter than any washing powder ever managed –
    happens to him 'as he prays'.
The suggestion is almost that this entry into the blinding glory of
    God is available to anyone who prays as Jesus did.

And what is the subject of his prayer?
The 'passing which he was to accomplish'.
The Greek word is *exodos*.
Jesus is on the point of making an Exodus as historic
    as Israel's journey from the slavery of Egypt
    to the freedom of the Promised Land.
It would be a painful process.
But it would end in glory.

One of the memories of Mount Tabor that I cherish
    is of a Mass celebrated in the basilica by our pilgrim group.
We had just been listening to the Gospel reading, and were still
    standing meditating in awe on the divine proclamation:
'This is my beloved Son'.
The solemn silence was finally broken by the voice of a child
    who had been fidgeting throughout the reading,
    and the basilica echoed to her tearful complaint:
    '*My* dad just told me off!'

Many people think of religion in general, and of Lent in particular,
    as a kind of telling off.
Today's Gospel is meant to reassure them
    that it's nothing of the kind.
God sees all of us, as he sees the praying Jesus on this Gospel page,
    as his beloved children.
'If only this experience could go on for ever',
    we say with the dazed disciples on the mountain.
Well, it will, but not yet.
'Tell no one,' Jesus says as the glorious moment passes.
Easter hasn't arrived yet.
There's still trouble ahead.
But at least we've had a glimpse of what lies beyond.

Further reflections

One of the things that I like most about Luke is the way he makes the Gospel stories his very own. They are not mere repetitions of Mark's and Matthew's texts. We believe he wrote some years later than them, and he certainly was not around when Jesus was alive. This means, therefore, that he thought a great deal about what he had been told, and about what he had observed in the young Christian community. Then, with a wonderful sense of freedom and conviction, he took his own particular slant on the stories told by witnesses. The account of the Transfiguration of Jesus was very much at the heart of Luke's faith. In fact, biblical scholars point out that Luke probably made the story the centre point of his Gospel on which the whole story of Jesus turns.

Luke devised a quite artificial framework for his Gospel, and placed events within sections that related to a number of journeys. The patterns are best understood when the Gospel is read as the first of two volumes. The themes are only completed in the Acts of the Apostles where the whole Christian community will go on a Christ-like journey to bring all people to the presence of God. Luke chose to omit three whole chapters of Mark so that he could make the Transfiguration the centre of an intricate theme. The pattern looks like this:

Mission of the twelve 9:1
    Passion foretold 9:21
        Transfiguration 9:28ff
    Passion foretold 9:44
Mission of the seventy-two 10:1

Luke wants us to understand that Jesus was able to undergo his Passion and death because he was a man of deep prayer and reflection. Luke, more than the other evangelists, seems aware of this aspect of Jesus' life. Mark and Matthew make the story of the Transfiguration sound as though Jesus set up the whole thing in order to show the disciples his glory. Luke, in saying that Jesus went up the mountain to pray, is suggesting that prayer can transfigure his readers too. This is certainly the experience of saints and mystics.

This week in Lent would be a good time for us to think about the way we pray. Is it the centre of our lives? I've recently written a book for schools about outstanding Christians. It is always humbling to research the lives of great people – especially those who base their lives on the teaching and example of Jesus. In one section I looked closely at Christians who made prayer the centre of their lives. The Russian archbishop, Anthony Bloom, explains prayer in these words: 'Prayer is born of the discovery that the world has depths; that we are not only surrounded by visible things but that we are also immersed in and penetrated by invisible things. And this invisible world is both the presence of God, the supreme, sublime reality, and our own deepest truth.' Jesus clearly experienced the deepest truth about himself when he touched the presence of God at the Transfiguration.

Luke is probably not marking Jesus out as the unique Son of God in this text; he is suggesting that we could all be transfigured by prayer and come into the presence of God. Great saints and mystics like Benedict, Teresa of Avila and Julian of Norwich left the crowded world to find stillness for their contemplative prayer. Lent is a time when we are invited to withdraw to the desert for contemplation too. It has to be said that for many people chance would be a fine thing! I remember reading an article in the *Tablet* some years ago where a senior social worker was aghast at the presumption in religious circles that the opportunities for retreats and quiet days of recollection were open to all. The people, she said, who needed this most were her clients – lone parents who struggle to survive and who live in crowded apartments with little money and never a chance of a baby-sitter. The *Tablet* article commented that very few people were responding to courses offered on social issues or on justice and poverty, whilst courses on prayer and spirituality were abundant and oversubscribed.

It is worth remembering that the Transfiguration story is only one description in the Gospel of a prayer experience. There are many ways of 'discovering that the world has depths' and of entering into the presence of God. There is, for example, the time when Jesus and his disciples were so busy that they didn't even have time to eat. Jesus suggested that they went off for a quiet weekend to 'a lonely place'. But the crowd guessed where they were heading and rushed to get there first. (Mark records the occasion in detail: Mark 6:30-34.) Now Jesus didn't say to the crowds, 'Go away, we need a time of quiet rest and reflection'; he responded to *their* needs and began to talk to them. That generous response is prayer too.

This came home to me many years ago when the children were very small. I wrote a diary entry called 'Night-time parents'. It went like this:

It is 5.30am and I'm not going to get any more sleep tonight because the children are up and about. They were very early to sleep last night as weeks of broken sleep finally caught up with them. First one, then the other, had chicken-pox, which meant many disturbed nights. Some nights I slept in three different beds. One night it was four, when I ended up in the spare room.

At 2am one morning, as I was cuddling a very itchy, miserable, spotted Blanca, it occurred to me that my friend Judith was probably also up, feeling far more grotty than I was, as she was still recovering from a difficult birth. And Ros, my neighbour was quite likely to be up too, as her children had chicken-pox as well. In fact there were probably hundreds of mums and dads in Norwich alone who would be up and about dabbing on calamine lotion, feeding the baby, giving doses of Calpol or cuddling little ones frightened by dreams. I know the members of some contemplative religious orders get up at night to praise God in the Prayer of the Church. We night-time parents make quite a community of prayer too.

We are encouraged to spend extra time at prayer during Lent. Exploring a Gospel text is, of course, a prayer in itself. We can reflect on the scene of the Transfiguration as Luke describes it, and then apply it to our own lives. Orthodox Christians may reflect on this text by standing silently before its icon. They believe that an icon reveals the presence of God. It puts the prayerful individual in contact with God in something of the way that Christ did. Paul called Christ the icon (image) of God: 'In him we see the God who can't be seen' (Colossians 1:15).

In 1980 the Catholic bishops of El Salvador wrote a letter to all their people, ending it with a reflection on this Gospel scene. They described Moses, Elijah, Peter, James and John as men who were capable of fighting, but who preferred peace to war. They said: 'Jesus channelled the aggression of those temperaments towards a rich work of construction, of building up justice and peace in the world. Let us ask the Divine Patron of El Salvador to transfigure in the same way the rich potential of this people.' In a similar way, the Anglican Bishop of Monmouth, Rowan Williams, used the Transfiguration scene to reflect on today's world. He noted that when the transfigured Jesus leaves the mountain he is confronted by a boy possessed by a demon. Rowan Williams goes on to comment that 6 August, the Feast of the Transfiguration, has become Hiroshima Day. 'Suicidal, diabolic sickness still waits at the bottom of the mountain, though now there are more bodies to look at.'

Another writer, Peter De Rosa, reflects that the light of the Transfiguration is inseparable from the darkness of pain and crucifixion. He wrote his meditation as a prayer:

Father, I thank you for this Gospel story
    which illustrates so well Christ's sovereignty.
I believe, Lord, that in everything he says and does
    he lights up and fulfils the law and the prophets;
    and it is enough to listen to him.
For Jesus is your Christ,
    even though death and dereliction

are waiting for him in Jerusalem.
It will be dark there,
    and on another hill, shaped like a skull,
    two other men will be beside him.
From his unclothed body, no light will radiate;
    and even you, Father, will be silent,
    except for the one Word you will be saying to us
    in the tremendous love of Jesus crucified.

Summary

Biblical scholars tell us that the story of the Transfiguration is central to Luke's Gospel. It was Mark and Matthew who first described the scene where Jesus took his three companions, Peter, John and James, up the mountain and was transfigured before them, in the presence of Moses and Elijah. Luke gives the story a different emphasis – he does not see it as an exhibition of Jesus's glory, but simply as an insight into prayer. The suggestion is that it is possible for anyone to enter into the blinding glory of God through prayer.

There are great saints and mystics who are proof of this: Benedict, Teresa of Avila and Julian of Norwich for example. But there are many ways of praying, and not all require solitude and the desert or the mountain. Busy people can find God in the midst of work, especially service to others. They will be the first to recognise that the presence of God is not always a comfortable, glorious experience; it is more likely to be touched by the cross – with a hint of the resurrection to come.

Photograph: Syndication International

Easter is ahead.

Discussion points

1. Compare the accounts of the Transfiguration in the three Gospels and note the differences: Mark 9:2-8; Matthew 17:1-8; Luke 9:28-36.

2. What do you understand by the word 'vision'? Is it an external, objective event or an internal experience?

3. Is there any difference between meditation and contemplation?

4. In your experience, are suffering and glory two sides of the same coin?

5. What does Anthony Bloom mean when he says, 'This invisible world is both the presence of God, the supreme, sublime reality, and our own deepest truth'?

Suggestions for action

During Lent we are encouraged to spend more time at prayer:

• Spend half an hour reading this Transfiguration text and apply the story to your own situation.

• Write your own prayer based on the text.

• Make a conscious effort to turn a busy, demanding day into a prayer. (If you meet as a group, share your experiences.)

Prayer

O God, early in the morning I cry to you.
Help me to pray
and concentrate my thoughts on you;
I cannot do this alone.

In me there is darkness,
but with you there is light;
I am lonely, but you do not leave me;
I am feeble in heart, but with you there is help;
I am restless, but with you there is peace.
In me there is bitterness, but with you there is patience;
I do not understand your ways,
but you know the way for me.

Dietrich Bonhoeffer (1906-1945)
'Morning Prayers', Christmas 1943

Week Three

God is patient

Reading for the third Sunday of Lent

It was just about this time that some people arrived and told him about the Galileans whose blood Pilate had mingled with that of their sacrifices. At this he said to them, 'Do you suppose that these Galileans were worse sinners than any others, that this should have happened to them? They were not, I tell you. No; but unless you repent you will all perish as they did. Or those eighteen on whom the tower of Siloam fell, killing them all? Do you suppose that they were more guilty than all the other people living in Jerusalem? They were not, I tell you. No; but unless you repent you will all perish as they did.'

He told this parable, 'A man had a fig tree planted in his vineyard, and he came looking for fruit on it but found none. He said to his vinedresser, "For three years now I have been coming to look for fruit on this fig tree and finding none. Cut it down: why should it be taking up the ground?" "Sir," the man replied, "leave it one more year and give me time to dig round it and manure it: it may bear fruit next year; if not, then you can cut it down."'

Luke 13:1-9

Today's Gospel reading comes as a bit of a shock.
True, the reading for the First Sunday of Lent
   was pretty strong on gloom and misery.
But last Sunday's reading reassured us that, during Lent
   God is not really telling us off.
What's all this then, today, about 'repent or perish'?
One is reminded of Mel Calman's dyspeptic God sitting on a cloud,
   and shouting, 'Behave, or I'll come down and do you!'

30

Well, yes, Lent is a time of contrasts.
It is always holding before our eyes the glory of Easter.
But it wouldn't be honest if it didn't also tell us
    that the only way to Easter is via Good Friday.
The prospect of life, joy and fulfilment is always being put before us.
But we're not to imagine we've already arrived.
There's still a way to go, and serious work to be done.
The Gospel calls this serious work 'repentance'.
In English, the word is harmless enough,
    and means little more than saying 'sorry'.
But in New Testament Greek, the word is much stronger:
    it means turning your ideas inside out,
    and seeing things from an entirely new angle.
And it's stronger still in Old Testament Hebrew,
    where the word for repentance is a metaphor
    for going into reverse gear.
It's what you do to a field when you plough it, or turn it upside down.
It's what you do to a glove when you've got it on wrong:
    you turn it inside out.

Few people repent as dramatically as this,
    in a once-in-a-lifetime manner.
For most of us, repentance is a daily exercise,
    needing to be repeated over and over again.
Nor is Jesus saying that God will zap the unrepentant.
In fact, in our Gospel reading, he is saying the very opposite.
Disasters happen to good people as well as to bad.
Remember, 'The rain falls on the just and on the unjust fella,
    but mostly on the just, since the unjust's nicked his umbrella.'

But if, given the kind of world we live in,
    disasters can happen to anyone, just or unjust, good or evil,
    shouldn't we remind ourselves, again and again, how
    desperately unprepared we are to come face to face with God?
Shouldn't the disasters we witness daily on TV and in the press
    act as a constant warning?

31

The story is told of the village which had so much rain
     that all its roads became flooded.
As the water reached windowsills,
     police and firemen made the round to lead people to safety.
Except one, who insisted that God would look after him.
As the water reached his upstairs rooms
     they brought a boat round to rescue him.
He still refused, saying he still put his trust in God.
Eventually he had to climb on to the roof,
     and the rescuers came with a helicopter, and threw him a rope.
'God will provide,' he stoutly insisted, and stayed on the roof.
Finally the flood engulfed even the roof,
     and the man was swept down into the water.
Angrily he shouted up at the God who had failed to rescue him.
God replied, 'But I came for you three times, and you refused.'

God is never absent. He is always present.
And not simply in the occasional extraordinary event,
     but in the most ordinary and daily.
And that presence of his is our saving.
He is not against us in our Lenten *Via Dolorosa*.
He is on our side. He does not condemn us.
Those who don't realise this may be condemning themselves.

The second half of today's reading makes this even clearer.
A fig tree has been occupying valuable space on the farm for years,
     and hasn't produced a thing.
Both Matthew and Mark curse it, and kill it off.
Luke (what a bringer of the Good News!) says,
     'Give it another chance. Perhaps next year. Who knows?'

We're not very good at producing fruits.
But God is infinitely patient. Thank God.

Further reflections

Patience. I'm not very good at it. I planted a delicate yellow rose over a new trellis nearly two years ago; it was supposed to have bloomed this summer (as I write), but there is no sign of a single blossom, only curled leaves, damaged by all the bad weather. I'm for digging it up and starting again, but the man at the garden centre assures me that it may come to flower next year. That's a long time to wait. (I'm clearly influenced by the instant garden make-overs so popular on television.) I'm just as impatient over home improvements. I find it very hard to put up with weeks of dust and disorder. I hope the family don't find me too disgruntled at such times! I ought to remind myself of the proverb: 'Patience is a bitter plant but it bears a sweet fruit.'

This week's Gospel reading should really fill us with enormous hope and relief, because it reminds us that God has infinite patience as he awaits our repentance from sin and stupidity. We do such crazy things to one another and to his world, creating unbelievable 'dust and disorder'. Yet Jesus assures us that God's patience is tireless; he never gives up on us. There is a story in the *Talmud* that illustrates the same point. Abraham invited an old man to his tent and expected him to join in prayer to the one true God. But the old man was a fire-worshipper, and on hearing this Abraham sent him away at once. That night God visited Abraham in a vision and said, 'I have put up with this ignorant man for 70 years. What right have you to send him away after just one night?'

Why is God so patient with us? Because he loves us. Love makes it possible to go on waiting and forgiving, however long it takes. For this reason, it is clearly easier to be patient with those close to us than it is to be patient with the stranger or outsider. Parents usually stand by their children no matter the cost. Soap viewers will recall how long it took Dot Cotton and Vera Duckworth to stop defending their ungrateful, selfish sons. They did finally give up on them; but we are assured that God will never give up on us. I recall a very sad discussion I had with a group of young offenders in Norwich Prison. I used to assist the prison chaplain and lead a fortnightly discussion group. I was eagerly assuring the young men that God forgives every offence without question. They said that this was too hard to believe. 'I'll believe in a God who forgives me when I am forgiven by society,' said one of my group. 'I know already that people won't give me a job when I get out, and my family won't have me back. If God is so loving, why doesn't he make it easier for us to be accepted when we want to change?'

The sorry reality is that we Christians are not always very good advertisements for God. Lent is a time when we should reflect on this and acknowledge what a bad job we make of things. It is time to say 'sorry' and start again. Acknowledging our failures and saying sorry is very difficult. I was most upset when I left the prison after that discussion. The men had admitted to me their crimes and expressed regret and sorrow for the hurt they caused. Yet they knew that many people would never forgive them. The most vocal youth revealed that his parents had given up on him. His sense of despair and lack of hope in any kind of future was shocking. Unlike the fig tree, he wasn't being given another chance. He felt he had been uprooted and thrown on the rubbish heap.

That meeting with disillusioned young offenders has stayed with me over the years. When I later became a parent I often shuddered at the thought of a child or youth feeling unforgiven and unloved by a mother or father. So it was with some anguish that I soon discovered how frail we all are, and how difficult it can be for us to say 'sorry'. In my diary I recorded a particularly dramatic day. Do you recall family days like this one?

Today was a bad day, a rather unhappy Sunday. I simply don't know what got into Pedro. First of all it began much too early. We put the clocks back last night, and I looked forward to that extra hour's sleep. No such luck! The children were up – and in lively mood – by 6am. By 9am I was very weary of their boisterous behaviour. By 10am I was nearly exhausted. It was one of those days when the phone rang as I was settling a squabble, and when friends called in at the very moment I had started the 'toilet, hand-wash, coats-on routine'.

This latter distraction turned Pedro from mildly co-operative to deliberately outrageous. It was a wonder that we all got to church in time for Mass. But I had made a big mistake. I had tried to impress on the children that today was special, and we needed to be particularly quiet and well-behaved. (Zoe and Andrea, three-year-old twins, friends of ours, were being baptised during the service, and Bert was helping out in the music group.) Pedro had other ideas. He whizzed his cars up and down the bench, then wriggled out and rushed to the porch, where he scooped Holy Water from a none-too-clean stoop into his mouth. Then he darted up the side aisle as he spotted another friend. I'd had enough, and asked Bert to leave the music to the others and take a defiant Pedro back home. 'I don't like church anyway,' he grumbled as he retreated.

When I arrived home with Blanca an hour later a voice shouted from the garden, 'And I'm not going to say "sorry".' At 3pm my neighbour, Ros, called in. 'Please,' she said, 'can Pedro and Blanca come and play? My three are driving me round the bend. I don't know what has got into them.' It was the answer to our problem. The five youngsters got down to playing happily together. The day's turmoil suddenly seemed forgotten. I was relieved, yet sad that neither Pedro nor I had found a way to say we were sorry. As I left Ros to return home Pedro ran after me and whispered, 'Mummy, it begins with an "s".'

I was the one who had been impatient with my boisterous son. He was the one to say 'sorry'. What a lesson for a mother to learn from her child! When we considered prayer last week, it was this kind of incident that I had in mind when I suggested that the presence of God can clearly shine through our most ordinary, even stressful, daily lives. It isn't any wonder that Jesus pointed out that the kingdom of God 'belongs' to little children (Luke 18:15-17). Children are more direct, and they live so much more in the present moment than we do. Our adult minds and lives get too cluttered up with non-essentials – which means we don't always see the obvious. Behind some of the Gospel conversations Jesus had with his apostles one can almost detect a sigh or groan – the patient teacher perplexed at the muddle-headed audience missing the point!

So let's try to clear our heads this Lent and get the point of the story. Bert put it in simple words, which are worth repeating:

God is never absent. He is always present.
And not simply in the occasional extraordinary event,
    but in the most ordinary and daily.
And that presence of his is our saving.
He is not against us in our Lenten *Via Dolorosa*.
He is on our side. He does not condemn us.
Those who don't realise this may be condemning themselves.

Summary

On first reading it may seem that God is threatening us with 'repent or perish'. Repentance is much more than saying 'Sorry'. In New Testament Greek it means turning things round, seeing things from a completely new angle. A few people do make a once-in-a-lifetime repentance, and their lives are dramatically changed. But most of us have to repent over and over again as we try to live after the example of Jesus.

The Gospel text does not, in fact, say that God will dispossess the unrepentant. The responsibility lies with ourselves. God is always on our side. If we don't realise this, we may condemn ourselves. God is infinitely patient with us. Luke once again adjusts the original story. Mark and Matthew had cursed the fig tree. But Luke is thinking of God's patience and simply says, 'Give it another chance. Perhaps next year.'

Lent is a good time to examine our daily lives to see how much 'turning around' we need before we reflect the love and patience of God to those around us. How else are they going to find God present in their midst?

Give it another chance.

37

Discussion points

1. Explore the different meanings of the word 'repentance'. How have you interpreted its meaning until now?

2. If disasters fall on the good and the bad alike, is God a fair and loving father?

3. Bert wrote: 'He (God) is on our side. He does not condemn us. Those who don't realise this may be condemning themselves.' What do you think he means by this?

4. How can Luke *change* earlier Gospel texts, written by Mark and Matthew? How can both versions of an original story be the Word of God?

5. In our lives 'God is never absent. He is always present.' How can troubled people, prisoners, the sick or the bereaved experience that this is true?

Suggestions for action

- **Prayer**
  Take time for a thorough and serious examination of conscience. Reflect on Psalm 103 (102).

- **Fasting**
  Give up some time to visit a friend/neighbour who is lonely or distressed.

- **Almsgiving**
  Find out more about local efforts to support ex-prisoners and/or the homeless. Offer a contribution to their work.

Prayer

Praise God who forgives all our sins,
and heals us of everything evil,
who rescues our life from the grave,
and clothes us in mercy and love.

Our God is all kindness and love,
so patient and so rich in pity,
not treating us as we deserve,
not paying us back for our sins.

As heaven is high above earth,
so strong is his love for his people;
as far as the east from the west,
so far he removes all our sins.

As fathers take pity on sons,
so God will show us his compassion,
for he knows of what we are made:
he knows we are no more than dust.

Psalm 103 (102):1-14

Week Four

Nothing is unforgivable

Reading for the fourth Sunday of Lent

The tax collectors and sinners were all crowding round to listen to him, and the Pharisees and scribes complained saying, 'This man welcomes sinners and eats with them.' So he told them this parable.

'There was a man who had two sons. The younger one said to his father, "Father, let me have the share of the estate that will come to me." So the father divided the property between them. A few days later, the younger son got together everything he had and left for a distant country where he squandered his money on a life of debauchery.

'When he had spent it all, that country experienced a severe famine, and now he began to feel the pinch; so he hired himself out to one of the local inhabitants, who put him on his farm to feed the pigs. And he would willingly have filled himself with the husks the pigs were eating, but no one would let him have them. Then he came to his senses and said, "How many of my father's hired men have all the food they want and more, and here I am dying of hunger! I will leave this place and go to my father and say: Father, I have sinned against heaven and against you; I no longer deserve to be called your son; treat me as one of your hired men." So he left the place and went back to his father.

'While he was still a long way off, his father saw him and was moved with pity. He ran to the boy, clasped him in his arms and kissed him. Then his son said, "Father, I have sinned against heaven and against you. I no longer deserve to be called your son." But the father said to his servants, "Quick! Bring out the best robe and put it on him; put a ring on his finger and sandals on his feet. Bring the calf we have been fattening, and kill it; we will celebrate by having a feast, because this son of mine was dead and has come back to life; he was lost and is found." And they began to celebrate.

'Now the elder son was out in the fields, and on his way back, as he drew near the house, he could hear music and dancing. Calling one of the servants he asked what it was all about. The servant told him, "Your brother has come, and your father has killed the calf we had been fattening because he has got him back safe and sound." He was angry then and refused to go in, and his father came out and began to urge him to come in; but he retorted to his father, "All these years I have slaved for you and never once disobeyed any orders of yours, yet you never offered me so much as a kid for me to celebrate with my friends. But, for this son of yours, when he comes back after swallowing up your property – he and his loose women – you kill the calf we had been fattening."

'The father said, "My son, you are with me always and all I have is yours. But it was only right we should celebrate and rejoice, because your brother here was dead and has come to life; he was lost and is found."'

Luke 15: 1-3, 11-32

Which is more shocking?
The suggestion made in the Church Lectionary later in the year
    that to save time the priest may omit this most shocking of
    Jesus' stories?
('After all, it is not as if it is a really important part of the Mass!')
Or the fact that we have heard the story so many times
    that it no longer shocks us?

What would Jesus' original audience have found so shocking about
    the story?
First, the brutal insensitivity of the younger son
    in demanding *now* the share due to him in his father's will.
He is equivalently telling his father, 'I wish you were dead.'
But the response of the father is equally shocking.

41

Instead of throwing the shameless lad out of the house
    as he deserves,
    he unbelievably hands over to him his share of the estate.
And instead of then washing his hands of such a wastrel son,
    he actually keeps such a weather-eye open for his return
    that he is able to see him 'when he was still a long way off'.
Most shocking of all, especially in a patriarchal setting
    where saving face is paramount,
    this totally love-crazed father throws all dignity to the wind
    as he runs down the village street, in full view of the public,
    to weep and hug and kiss and welcome home
    this swineherd of a son.
An Arab bishop assured me that *no* Palestinian father
    would ever demean himself to such an extent.

Jesus told his stories to correct the false images of God
    we keep making for ourselves.
We had imagined God as an issuer of 'thou shalt nots',
    a cold law-maker and a calculating law-enforcer.
But he is nothing of the kind,
    as even page after page of the Old Testament had already shown.
He is even more spendthrift than his prodigal children,
    forgiving them unconditionally in the most irrational way,
    and refusing to hold their worst excesses against them.
Even the suggestion of repentance is brushed aside.
What a shock!
Having a God like that comes pretty close to having no God at all!

But there is an even worse shock to come.
Conscious of our own waywardness,
    we listen to the story and humbly beat our breast
    as we identify with the younger son.
'Amazing grace, how sweet the sound.'
But the whole point of the story,
    as the opening verses of the reading make clear,
    is the attitude of the *elder* son –

why do we so often leave this bit out? –
bitter, angry and resentful over a father
who can be so scandalously tolerant,
and so irresponsibly extravagant with the family estate.
And so the real shock of the story only registers
when we realise the extent to which that resentment
is nestling somewhere deep in our own hearts.
'Of course we are all unworthy and undeserving.
But surely there are some who are more undeserving
of God's attention than we are!'

The fact is that there are not.
It is precisely the most undeserving who are closest to God's heart.
That is the sort of God he is.
To resent that is to be even more lost and distant from God
than the younger son had been.
This does not mean that the elder son is a villain.
He is only blind.
The story therefore comes to its climax
when the father pleads with him (and through him with us)
to open our eyes and see him as he really is,
and as the younger son has already seen him.
For him, such a father is sheer joy.
For him, being treated as a son
has given him a chance of *becoming* one.

Luther said that if we had nothing of the New Testament except this
parable, we would have the complete Gospel.

Further reflections

I do find it remarkable that this extraordinary parable is only recorded by Luke. What happened to the other evangelists? Did they decide to leave it out? The scholars suggest that Luke was using a new source of material unknown to the others. That seems strange to me. How could those early disciples, who repeated, over and over, the stories that Jesus told, leave this one out or lose it? Maybe its message was just too shocking to believe. A God who forgives without any conditions? Impossible!

We already noticed last week that Luke felt he had to add a sentence to the parable of the fig tree, because the original story did not reflect the infinite patience of God. Here he is again determined to show the infinite mercy and compassion of God. Forgiveness is central to the teaching of Jesus. Luke saw this as a most profound insight, and it is hardly surprising that he is later the only evangelist to put the words of forgiveness on the lips of the dying Jesus: 'Forgive them, Father! They don't know what they are doing.' One very profitable Lenten task would be to explore the theme of forgiveness in Luke's Gospel. You may get a surprise.

I sometimes set my students the task of reflecting on God's attitude to sin and the sinner. We first of all consider the possible attitudes God could take. Then, in groups, the class decides which attitude they think was expressed in the Gospels.

These are the various responses that God could make to sin:

(a) He could explode in anger, outraged that his plans have been upset.

(b) He could be rather more controlled, weigh up the harm done and demand strict satisfaction.

(c) He could be generous enough to ask nothing more than an acknowledgement of guilt and a promise to reform.

(d) He could turn a complete blind eye and act as if nothing was wrong, offering total, unconditional forgiveness.

I have discovered that most Christians seem to believe that God's response is (c). My students have pointed out that the Catholic practice of 'Confession', or Sacrament of Reconciliation as we call it, assumes that response. The Sacrament requires a confession of guilt, an act of contrition, and a promise to do better in the future. Christians seem genuinely surprised to discover that the Gospel writers, in particular Luke, opt for (d). The parable of the prodigal son is told to make just this point. It is the father in the story who is the 'prodigal' one. As Bert has already described, the father's action is almost beyond belief in its boldness and extraordinary generosity.

Luke's point is that Jesus was convinced his Father forgives, not because people repent, or believe, or earn it, but quite simply because God is good. 'Well,' you might say, 'Jesus did say to sinners, "Go and sin no more".' He did. But according to this text, although he always invited sinners to repent, he never demanded that they should. Today's parable insists that God forgives without any conditions. He forgives before the sinner even considers repentance. We find this hard to believe because so few people ever achieve such generosity of spirit.

A few do, however, and they astonish us. Gordon Wilson, who survived the bomb at Enniskillen but lost his beloved daughter Marie, amazed the world when he told the BBC reporter at his hospital bedside that he bore no ill will towards the bombers. He did not pretend to understand God's purpose in the terrible tragedy, but accepted it as part of God's greater plan. Some people thought that he would eventually break down, and show some anger or bitterness towards those who had caused his family so much pain. But his sense of forgiveness was undiminished ten years later when he died.

Unconditional forgiveness is not easy. It also creates a moral dilemma. There is a real tension between offering forgiveness to the sinner, and at the same time showing compassion for the victim. If God does not find this a problem, we certainly do. Many of you will be familiar with the story of Sister Helen Prejean whose book was made into the film *Dead Man Walking*. Her book describes the drama of being involved as spiritual adviser to prisoners on death row. The film is a powerful portrayal of the struggle that Sister Helen underwent in standing alongside the murderer, Matthew Poncelet, whilst she felt overwhelming compassion for the extreme suffering of the victims' families. Helen was aware that the parents 'may feel that the refusal to demand death, the harshest punishment possible, would be a betrayal of their daughter's (or son's) memory'. However, she became convinced that justice must always be based on mercy. Healing, forgiveness and reconciliation must always be a possibility. This is not offered in capital punishment.

Another recent attempt to bring the offender and the offended together was made in South Africa after the ending of apartheid and the election of Nelson Mandela as president. An enquiry was set up into the human rights abuses that played such a large part in recent history. The Truth and Reconciliation Commission, chaired by Archbishop Desmond Tutu, required all those who had committed crimes against humanity to seek amnesty. They had to appear in public and confess their actions. By doing this, it was hoped they would be forgiven and reconciled with those they had oppressed. Throughout the hearings, Archbishop Tutu wept at the scale of suffering described by witnesses. Yet he still advocated mutual forgiveness and reconciliation. Proof of the difficulty of the task lies in the fact that it was not entirely successful. But at least an attempt was made to act in a way that was rooted in a Christian appreciation of forgiveness. (It has to be noted that the Commission found the Christian Churches guilty on many charges of injustice and prejudice.)

We may come to the conclusion this week that the lesson of the parable is too idealistic by far! Who can forgive without question and without demands? As I am writing this chapter, this is an issue that is being discussed in the national press. It has been made public that a priest paedophile, now serving a prison sentence, was given a second chance to work in a pastoral role, after some form of treatment and counselling. Although this happened many years ago, before medical psychology had come to a deeper understanding of paedophilia, Archbishop Murphy-O'Connor is accused by many of weakness and total irresponsibility for not handing the priest over to the police at once. What a difficult position for a Christian leader to be in. Are there sins too evil for forgiveness and reconciliation? How much notice should be taken of the wider community and especially the suffering of the victims? The Archbishop had his eye on the Gospel. The public would prefer that he keep his feet on the ground. How do we solve such difficult questions? Who knows! But it would be a good thing for us to refuse to 'take sides', and to offer compassion towards all those involved and hurt by such tragic incidents.

Summary

We are used to reading this parable and generally think of it as a good example of the sinner returning home to the embrace of his father. It is a good preparation story for the Sacrament of Reconciliation, when we ask God's forgiveness and resolve never to sin again. But the story is, in fact, a shocking one. And one that would have astonished Jesus' audience.

It is the Father who is prodigal; he is so tolerant and forgiving that it is a scandal. The story should really focus on the attitude of the elder son, who is angry at his father's unconditional love and forgiveness of the lazy, selfish younger brother. Luke delights in presenting us with this picture of God who forgives without any conditions attached. A close study of his Gospel shows that Jesus preaches again and again this unique message: God, his Father, forgives not because people repent, or believe, or earn it, but quite simply because God is good.

This is a very difficult lesson to learn, and few achieve such heroic forgiveness and compassion. We catch glimpses of it in the lives of Christians like Gordon Wilson, Sister Helen Prejean and Archbishop Tutu. But we all know how easy it is to react like the elder son, and demand that God be less generous when *we* are hurt by the sinful actions of others.

Photograph: UNWRA

God forgives simply because he is good.

Discussion points

1. When you read the parable of the prodigal son, with which of the characters do you identify? Why?

2. Do you think it is possible to be as unconditional in forgiveness as the father is?

3. 'For him [the younger son], being treated as a son has given him a chance of *becoming* one.' What did Bert mean by this?

4. Look again at the four possible responses that God could make to sin (page 44). Do you find it strange that the Gospel opts for (d) but the Church suggests (c) is more appropriate? Why would this be?

5. Do you think that there are some sins that are too evil for unconditional forgiveness? If so, does this mean that the teaching of Jesus is simply too idealistic?

Suggestions for action

- Search Luke's Gospel for all references to forgiveness.

- Read *Dead Man Walking* or borrow the video of the film. Discuss with your family or group the moral issues it presents.

- Pray this week for all those in positions of authority: judges, magistrates, bishops, teachers and social workers who often have to make judgements on the appropriate treatment of offenders.

Prayer

If you really love, then when you love
you are really doing what you like.
When you keep quiet, do it out of love;
when you cry out, do it out of love;
when you correct someone, do it out of love;
when you forgive someone, do it out of love.
Let your life be utterly rooted in love:
from this root, nothing but good can grow.

St Augustine (354-430)

Week Five

Go and sin no more

Reading for the fifth Sunday of Lent

And Jesus went to the Mount of Olives. At daybreak he appeared in the Temple again; and as all the people came to him, he sat down and began to teach them.

The scribes and Pharisees brought a woman along who had been caught committing adultery; and making her stand there in the middle they said to Jesus, 'Master, this woman was caught in the very act of committing adultery, and in the Law Moses has ordered us to stone women of this kind. What have you got to say?' They asked him this as a test, looking for an accusation to use against him. But Jesus bent down and started writing on the ground with his finger. As they persisted with their question, he straightened up and said, 'Let the one among you who is guiltless be the first to throw a stone at her.' Then he bent down and continued writing on the ground. When they heard this they went away one by one, beginning with the eldest, until the last one had gone and Jesus was left alone with the woman, who remained in the middle. Jesus again straightened up and said, 'Woman, where are they? Has no one condemned you?' 'No one, sir,' she replied. 'Neither do I condemn you,' said Jesus. 'Go away, and from this moment sin no more.'

John 8:1-11

This last Lenten reading before Holy week
    is apparently not from Luke,
    but from the Gospel of John.
I say 'apparently' because, although the story is preserved
    in a number of ancient manuscripts of John's Gospel,
    it is omitted by an even larger number of them.
Most scholars agree that it is not in fact a 'John' story,
    and there is reason to believe that it is a misplaced 'Luke' story.
Certainly it is in congenial company
    with the stories Luke has told us through the whole of Lent.

This prodigal daughter of Israel makes a good pair
    with last week's prodigal son.
Both of them reveal a God who is even more prodigal
    than they have been!
And given the guilt-ridden mentality of so many Christians,
    (we Catholics are the worst –
    is it a case of bad conscience or of bad teaching?)
    this free forgiveness of God needs to be emphasised even more
    than the sinfulness of sin.

At the heart of the Gospel, this story tells us,
    stands a God who does not condemn, make retribution,
    or punish; he simply forgives over and over again.
When Peter asked Jesus: 'How many times should I forgive people
    who have done me down? Go on, I'll be generous.
    As many as seven times?'
Jesus replied, 'Not enough! More like seventy times seven!
    In short, every time it's needed.'
Why? Because that's how God forgives.
Whatever it is that you've done, he will *not* condemn you.
He'll forgive even that.
His attitude is not one of reproof, or disapproval, or condemnation.
His attitude is only one of pity.
'Neither do I condemn you. Go and sin no more.'
At the end of our Gospel story

there are only two characters left on the stage:
one is pitiable, and the other is all pity;
one is heartbroken, the other all heart.

In the memorable Russian film *Andrei Rublev*, the artist is commissioned to fill the apse of a new church with an overpowering mural of Judgement.
His sponsors describe the kind of thing they have in mind,
and urge him to put in scenes that will put the fear of God in everyone.
The apse remains empty for months, while Rublev and his team of painters agonise over the task.
Finally the commissioners return, and demand to know why there is no progress on their 'Judgement' scene.
An embarrassed Rublev replies,
'Because I can't see what it has to do with the Gospel'.

Rublev's insight is central.
At the heart of the Gospel stands the cross,
where the Son of God does not blast his enemies to hell,
but forgives them.
'That is what my Father does,' he adds.
'Just accept that, and your whole life will change'.
What he is saying is that when we finally arrive at the gates of Paradise we will see the notice that is posted there:
'Trespassers Will Be Forgiven.'
That's what heaven is all about!
A famous medieval epitaph reads:
Here lies Martin Elginbrodde
Have mercy on my soul, dear God,
As I would do if I were God
And you were Martin Elginbrodde.
What a nonsense to imagine God could be any less forgiving than I'd be!

Commentators have speculated about what exactly it was
　　that Jesus' finger was writing in the dust
　　while everyone was pointing
　　an accusing finger at the woman.
Some suggest it was the sins of each one of them,
　　and that this was why they slunk off one by one.
Others say he could have been writing down his decision on the case,
　　in the manner of the Roman judges of the time.
But surely it is more likely that Jesus was quite deliberately
　　opting out of the condemnatory attitude of everyone else,
　　and simply doodling on the ground as much as to say,
　　'Include me out.'

Which isn't to be taken to mean that Jesus is turning a blind eye
　　to the woman's misdemeanour.
On the contrary, the advice he gives her is clear:
　　'Go, and sin no more.'
But what he says immediately before that is even clearer:
　　'Neither do I condemn you.'
In other words: 'I'm doing what God does: he forgives.
　　Now go and do likewise.'

Further reflections

This week's reading is re-enforcing last week's message. We are reminded again and again that God forgives without any questions being asked. We need to tell ourselves this over and over again, because forgiveness doesn't come very easily to us. Like the Scribes and Pharisees in the story, we are very quick to point the finger and lay the blame. It is a reaction to get ourselves out of trouble. We learn this very quickly in life, as any parent or infant school teacher will tell you!

When our children were small I remember making a big mistake. I shouted out from the kitchen, in accusing voice, 'Who spilt the milk?' 'She did,' shouted Pedro. 'He did,' shouted Blanca. The Adam and Eve syndrome. I've realised over the years that this kind of confrontation is counter-productive. Lies can be avoided if the adults aren't so threatening. I should have said (calmly), 'Hello, the milk got spilt. Will one of you come and help me clear it up?' That kind of question usually gets a positive response and an accurate explanation. And we all feel better.

I learnt that lesson many years ago in school and I never forgot the occasion. There was a lot of frustrated talk in the staff room about a girl who was always in trouble. This time she had 'stolen' a pair of gloves from someone's coat pocket. 'I know they belong to Anne,' said one of the teachers, 'but she flatly denies it.' I felt very protective towards the accused girl, Maria, because she was in my class, and I happened to know that she was going through an appalling situation at home. I felt compelled to protect her. I bought a new pair of gloves. I created a situation where Maria was with me alone. Then I casually said, 'Oh Maria, could you do with a pair of gloves? I don't need these and I noticed that you had to borrow a pair the other day.' Without hesitation, Maria grabbed this escape route. 'Thanks,' she said. 'Yes, I did find a pair in the cloakroom. Shall I give them back to you?' I vowed, from that day on, that I would try never to put a youngster in such a corner that she could only defend herself by lies.

I wish I always had the patience to keep to my good intention, because I know it pays off. It certainly diffused many a potential argument when the children were small. But I had to smile at the ultra-honesty it produced. I remember once when Pedro came in to the room as I was getting dressed and suggested that I go and have a look in the kitchen. I found a chocolate wrapper on the table. 'I ate it,' he announced, with a broad grin.

You may have noticed that I like to avoid confrontation, and this could be a rather selfish motive for offering forgiveness and showing compassion. I would love to think that Jesus sat quietly on the ground, doodling in the dust, for the same reason! But I doubt it. He was showing a profound insight into the heart of God that had never been fully understood before. His Jewish brethren were responding to their own Law and practice when they suggested stoning the woman caught committing adultery. They had a way of dealing with sinners: 'An eye for an eye, and a tooth for a tooth.' Our tabloid newspapers suggest that this mentality is the common one and should therefore be revived: bring back the death penalty; castrate the rapist; flog the thief.

But the message of the Gospel is clear: God is not like that. He does not seek retribution. When Jesus quietly addressed the crowd as they threatened the woman with a deadly punishment, he not only introduced a compassionate response to sin, he also challenged the Religious Law. It was a bold and dangerous move; religious leaders do not like to be confronted in this way. The text says that this whole incident was set up anyway, because they were 'looking for an accusation to use against him'. This was not the first time that he had taught a new message and challenged the old ways.

Love your enemies,
do good to those who hate you,
bless those who curse you,
and pray for those who ill-treat you.
If anyone hits you on one cheek,
let him hit the other one too;
if someone takes your coat,

let him have your shirt as well . . .
Do not judge others,
and God will not judge you;
do not condemn others,
and God will not condemn you;
forgive others,
and God will forgive you.

Luke 6:27-29, 37

This is a very strong message for us to consider this Lent. It is unambiguous and quite extraordinary in its demands. Are we really supposed to take Jesus seriously? In a book written for Lent, *Good Friday People*, Sheila Cassidy considers this same question. She writes:

> My commonplace book is full of quotes, gathered from all over the world. My favourite is this Jewish saying, heard on the radio: 'We must meet extravagant and unreasonable hatred with an extravagant and unreasonable love.' What he is saying is, we must love like God: unconditionally, unilaterally, and for ever. John of the Cross knew all about God's love: 'Where there is no love,' he said, 'sow love – and you will reap love.' Fine, but I like better the very pragmatic modification of the starry-eyed Carmelite's aphorism by a pragmatic Dominican working in the Peace Camps in Israel. 'Where there is no love,' he says, 'sow love, and *somebody* will reap love.'

One final thought for our Lenten journey. We have been considering the unconditional forgiveness of God. Where does this leave our Christian doctrine of heaven and hell? We must surely consider the possibility that hell has to be empty! Julian of Norwich said that in her visions she certainly saw no one there. In the sayings of the Hasidim we may have an answer to this perplexing question:

At the Last Judgement,
God will bring you into his presence one by one,
and there he will tell you
what your life was really about.
Then you will understand
the good you did and the bad.
And the good you did will be heaven,
and the bad your hell.
And then God will forgive you.

I don't know about you, but this delightful reflection moves my Lent fast forward to Easter.

Summary

Although this reading is from John's Gospel, most scholars agree that it isn't really a 'John' story. It is more likely to be a misplaced 'Luke' story. For Luke repeats over and over again Jesus' message that God forgives the sinner with unconditional pardon and compassion. In this particular story of the woman caught in adultery, Jesus challenges the Law that demands precise punishment for sin. He is bold to question the Jewish tradition of 'an eye for an eye'. But Jesus is consistent in his preaching. At the heart of his message is the revelation that God does not condemn, make retribution or punish. God forgives over and over again. If we base our lives on the Gospel, meditating on Jesus' teaching, we will, hopefully, learn to forgive with such generosity. We can see examples of Christians who have learnt from the Gospel – Rublev who could not paint an angry God; Julian of Norwich who could not see anyone in hell. But the lesson we need to learn is a hard one. When Jesus describes to us how God acts, he says: 'Now go and do likewise.'

Photograph: UNWRA

'Neither do I condemn you.'

Discussion points

1. What do you make of the biblical scholarship that casts doubt on where the Gospel stories come from?

2. If you were an artist how would you portray God in a mural of the Judgement?

3. Is there some unresolved tension for Christians when dealing with misbehaviour or downright evil?

4. Choose a hypothetical incident of bad behaviour in your family or workplace. List the ways the incident could be handled. Discuss this with a group.

5. Read the Sermon on the Mount (Matthew 5:38-47 or Luke 6:29-30). Suggest actual situations that correspond to the recommendations. Would Jesus' way actually 'work'?

Suggestions for action

- Read and reflect prayerfully on the Sermon on the Mount. Read and reflect prayerfully on this week's Gospel reading. Make one very firm resolution.

- If you can find a copy of Sheila Cassidy's *Good Friday People* (Darton, Longman & Todd, 1991) it is well worth reading during Holy Week.

- On a large sheet of card draw the outline of a cross. During the coming week cut out from the papers clippings or pictures of people who are suffering in any way. Glue them inside your cross. If you are working as a group conclude your meeting with prayers for these people. How else could you help them?

Prayer

Today it is very easy
to point out the injustice of others.
But how few cast a glance at their own conscience!
How easy it is to denounce structural injustice,
institutionalised violence, social sin!
It is true this sin is everywhere,
but where are the roots of this social sin?
In the heart of every human being.
We are all sinners.
Salvation begins with the human person.
And in Lent this is God's call:
Be converted!

Oscar Romero (1917-1980)

Conclusion _____

An account of the Passion and death of Jesus probably existed before the first Gospel was written. The first thirteen chapters of Mark are no more than a long introduction to this most dramatic week in the life of Jesus. The Gospels of Matthew, Luke and John follow the pattern set by Mark, and similarly focus the reader's attention on the events that unfolded from Palm Sunday onwards.

The Gospel of Luke (from which our readings are taken) is particularly keen to show the whole of Jesus' life as one continual journey to that final week in Jerusalem, which is celebrated by all Christian traditions as Holy Week. The Palm Sunday procession, the Maundy Thursday Eucharist, the Good Friday Veneration of the Cross, and the Holy Saturday Vigil are so rich in word, action and symbolism that they hardly need any further commentary. We hope that our reflections on the five Sundays leading up to that final week will help Christians to enter more deeply into the Easter mystery of Christ on the cross, risen in glory.

Christ on the cross,
    not crushed by death,
    but broken by his love too deep for knowing.
Christ on the cross,
    not crushed by death,
    but living on in love too deep for crushing.

Christ on the cross,
    not slain for sin,
    but broken by his love too great for giving.
Christ on the cross,
    not crushed by death,
    but living on in love too great for slaying.

Christ on the cross,
   not killed by man,
   but broken by his love too strong for holding.
Christ on the cross,
   not crushed by death,
   but living on in love too strong for killing.
C. R.

To believe in the risen Christ
   is to believe in the person of Jesus of Nazareth
   whose whole life proclaimed a God of love and mercy.
To believe in the risen Christ is to believe
   that this reality was not extinguished at death,
   and that Jesus' love and forgiveness
   were stronger than the forces which killed him.
To believe in the risen Christ
   is to know that he who was foolish and weak
   became the wisdom and power of God.
To believe in the risen Christ is to believe
   that on the cross God endorsed Jesus
   as the person he had shown himself to be
   throughout his life.

To believe in the resurrection
   means that for me Jesus is not a mere memory;
   he continues to live by the power of God,
   and to speak to me across the frontiers of death.
To believe in the resurrection
   means that I have committed myself
   to the God revealed to me in Jesus' death,
   and that he has shown me the face of the living Christ.
To believe in the resurrection
   means that I acknowledge the crucified Jesus
   as governing the manner of my life.

The resurrection means
   that Jesus is the resurrection of the body.
The resurrection means
   that Jesus lives on with such a fullness of life
   that he is able to animate a whole community of people.
The resurrection means
   that I have seen Jesus return to life
   and appear in the least of his brethren.
The resurrection means
   that in Jesus, and especially in his death,
   I have understood the purpose of my life.
The resurrection means
   that Jesus constantly comes into my life.

H. J. R.